The *Simple* Answer and Solution to our Housing and Economic Crisis

Are You Spending Money You Don't Have?

Wyatt Abbitt

authorHOUSE®

AuthorHouse™
1663 Liberty Drive, Suite 200
Bloomington, IN 47403
www.authorhouse.com
Phone: 1-800-839-8640

First published by AuthorHouse   2/16/2009

ISBN: 978-1-4389-5519-3 (e)
ISBN: 978-1-4389-5518-6 (sc)

Library of Congress Control Number: 2009901364

Printed in the United States of America
Bloomington, Indiana

This book is printed on acid-free paper.

Contents

Introduction	3
The Problem	5
My Personal Experience	17
Who's to Blame?	31
The Solution	43
Summary	69

Introduction

Lately I have been fascinated with the recent news related to the housing market and overall economy. We have seen mortgages in foreclosure, families in bankruptcy, banks and other financial institutions fail, builders and other contractors fail, and panic spread throughout our economy. I desperately want to scream out, "Didn't anyone see this coming?" Or I think the more appropriate question would be "Why did we choose to ignore it?" We let greed cloud our judgment: let's make a dollar today and worry about the effects of our superfast growth rate tomorrow.

It was apparent to me a few years ago that the housing bubble would burst and come crashing down. I think everyone else knew it too but decided to stay the course anyway. I knew that the explosive growth couldn't be normal, but like everyone else I ignored my gut instinct and tried to make some money. I made a few risky decisions that could have been disastrous. Thankfully, my decisions only taught me a lesson, but I know how easy it was and still is to become one of the victims of the recent housing market collapse.

I am not an economist, banker, politician, or expert in any manner; I'm just an average working American concerned with our economy and how it will look in the future. I am also concerned with the people we elect to run our government, but I will save most of those thoughts for another book. I was tired of listening to the so-called experts and politicians talk about the problems with the housing market and our economy, so I decided to talk about the issues from my perspective. I thought, how could my point of view be wrong? None of the so-called experts agree with each other.

I work for a global distributor of building materials, so I know firsthand the devastation our economy has faced and will continue to face in the months or even years to come. I did not conduct extensive research or ask for many opinions before writing this book. I am just putting my own thoughts down on paper to vent a little and in hopes that someone may benefit from my opinions and experiences. I am also not an English professor, so please excuse any grammatical errors. Also, if you like my book, please recommend it to someone else, preferably the president of the United States if you happen to know him. If you don't like my book, I apologize, and please make sure to recycle when you throw it out.

The Problem

In order to find a solution, we must first identify the problem. Most people seem to overanalyze or overcomplicate the situation and lose sight of the simple problem—and that's what it really is, a simple problem created by simple issues. Unfortunately, it was a simple problem whose impact had a domino effect on the housing and financial market and led to a major economic crisis. No one will ever agree on the economy or how things are related, but to me it seems like one simple issue is the root cause of our housing and financial crisis. I will discuss several key factors I feel fueled or led to the housing market's sharp rise and dramatic fall, but the main problem was cash.

Cash Flow - The main problem is cash, or lack of cash, to be more specific. Obviously, there are many factors influencing our housing and economic crisis, but in my opinion, people's inability to make the mortgage payments on their homes by far represents the largest share of the problem. People were buying homes they could not afford. As buyers became delinquent on their mortgage payments, we saw home foreclosures on a mass scale. These home foreclosures started the snowball that's still rolling today. This is the root cause of our current housing and economic crisis.

Whether at work or at home, we don't seem to be concerned with saving money or paying in advance anymore but are now focused on the almighty monthly payment. We are leveraging our finances to the furthest point possible. Any little hiccup can be disastrous. The thought process now is what can I buy today and pay for tomorrow? Better yet, what can I buy today and pay for over the next one, two, ten, or thirty years? This notion may work well for some people and businesses but can backfire easily when monthly payments exceed monthly income. This notion also requires continual growth to produce cash and stay ahead of the debt curve. Too many buyers focused on the monthly payment and for whatever reason miscalculated what they could afford. People just didn't have enough cash to pay for their homes.

Financing for consumer purchases or business functions is a very important and necessary part of our economy. It allows us to buy things now versus saving up and buying later. The more expensive the purchase, the more necessary the financing becomes. This is most notably common when buying a house. If we were required to pay for a house up front, most people would rent forever. Only the superrich could afford to buy a home before the age of retirement. My point here is that I understand the importance of financing. Our problem is not financing but the thought that financing is good for all occasions and has no limits. Debt is OK but becomes a problem when not balanced or managed properly.

Many experts or retailers will tell you that debt is good, and you should never pay cash up front for anything. If interest rates are low, you should finance your purchase and invest your money. For example, you have $1,000 in hand and are getting ready to buy a $1,000 TV. You have a choice to pay in full up front or finance your purchase. Let's say you're eligible to receive a consumer loan with an 11 percent annual percentage rate (APR). Theoretically, you are better off financing the TV and using your cash to invest in something bringing you more than an 11 percent annual return. At least that's what the experts say. Now, a little dose of reality. No one does this! Or at least very, very few do. Most people will finance the TV and spend the $1,000 in cash somewhere else. So that deal wasn't quite as good as it sounded in theory. Especially since the price of that TV (depending on the loan terms) just increased by 10, 20, maybe 40 percent! Either decision is still good for the economy, but simple decisions like this are what lead to potential problems. This causes people to become too leveraged. What happens is people start thinking about what else they can buy now and pay for later. Or even worse, what happens when people start using credit cards to pay for these types of purchases but never pay down the principal? Many people just make the minimum payment on their credit card, which only covers the interest. When do they reach the point of no more spending and focus on paying down the principal balance? This type of thinking can get people in trouble if spending is not controlled and debt is not managed properly.

As long as I can make the monthly payment, the purchase is good, right? Wrong! People are buying things they cannot afford or buying more than they can afford. It's easy to lose sight of what you should or shouldn't buy or what's actually affordable when you are using a monthly payment to gauge what you can afford to buy. Purchases still need to be proportionate to your overall disposable income. For example, I was once the target of a boat salesman trying to sell me a boat that I knew I couldn't afford. Just for fun my wife and I decided to stop by a boat dealership to do a little window shopping. We were of course quickly approached by one of the sales associates, who tried very hard to sell us a boat. He was very convincing and clever in promoting the fifteen-year financing that was available. Of course a special interest rate was available for that weekend only. The monthly payment was actually affordable to me, but the total purchase would have been more than my annual salary. I wasn't in the poor house at the time but certainly didn't need to be spending that much money on a boat—especially when you consider the maintenance cost, storage cost, insurance, and gas it would take to own and operate the boat. With the current gas prices, you could have doubled or even tripled that monthly payment we discussed. Although I didn't purchase the boat, I understand how easy it is to fool yourself into thinking you can afford more than you actually can. I certainly could have paid for the boat each month, but if I ever decided to use it, I would not have been able to afford to buy clothes, go out to dinner, or spend my money on some of the luxury-type items that are a desired part of any normal lifestyle. Most of these luxury-type items are underestimated or completely left out of most budgeting discussions. This is why it's so easy for people to overestimate their buying power and underestimate their spending habits or needs.

As you can see, too much focus on what you can afford via a monthly payment can be dangerous. People need to focus on what they should buy and when and why. Spending your monthly income on a house you can afford may be a great decision. Spending your monthly income on a nonessential item may not be the best decision. People should consider purchasing nonessential items with cash or on a short-term payment basis. You never know what your future cash flow position will be, so make sure to limit your exposure and choose your payment options wisely. Financing will limit your future disposable income, as you will be committed to monthly payments for the term of your loan.

The housing market was very attractive from 2000 to 2005 and many people were in the market to buy. The market saw first-time buyers and lots of people wanting to buy bigger. This was great for the economy, but there seemed to be one common theme with buyers. Their focus was on the initial monthly payment, and that initial monthly payment was the main determining factor in what they could afford to buy. There were lots of new financing options available, so buyers were able to receive larger than normal loans for more expensive homes. These financing options were great for buyers whose income was expected to rise sharply over the next few years but potentially dangerous for others. Some buyers were shortsighted as they planned to refinance or sell the house prior to the lower rate expiring. They were depending on their home values continuing to rise. Other buyers were uninformed and didn't fully understand their mortgage agreements. They didn't understand that the low initial rate was temporary and didn't understand the consequences of a rate increase. Either way, too many buyers became stuck with houses they didn't have the money to pay for, which is the main reason we are in this mess.

<u>Lenders (banks and mortgage companies)</u> – This brings up the question of budgeting and the question a lot of buyers were asking their lenders: "Why did my payment skyrocket?" For a lot of people, their payments skyrocketed due to the rate on their adjustable rate mortgage, or ARM, loan expiring and becoming variable or fixed at a higher rate. Unlike a thirty-year fixed-rate mortgage, where your rate stays the same for the term of the loan, an ARM will change after a specified period of time. This time frame could be three, five, or ten years. Your rate will then become variable and base itself on an agreed-upon market indicator. In most cases, this indicator is the prime rate. Most agreements will specify that the new rate on your mortgage will be prime plus 1, 2, or 3 percent. The prime rate is variable and could fluctuate from month to month. Most agreements have caps on the rate increase but can still rise to a point that will significantly raise the monthly mortgage payment. Too many lenders failed to explain the details to new or uninformed buyers who didn't quite understand the objective or the consequences of an ARM loan. Instead, they offered a low up-front "teaser rate" to entice buyers to purchase a more expensive home. Buyers who didn't understand the ARM loan or who underestimated the potential payment increase when the fixed portion of the ARM expired faced major payment shock when the new, higher variable rate kicked in.

Many buyers in this situation couldn't afford the higher payments and defaulted on their loans.

While some buyers didn't understand the ARM loan, others did and planned to refinance with a fixed-rate mortgage prior to the ARM turning into a variable-rate mortgage. Well, little did everyone know that home prices would soon drop significantly, and this decline would pose a major obstacle to refinancing. Buyers who didn't have enough equity in their homes soon found themselves owing more than the homes were worth. This is called reverse, or negative, equity. Lenders would not refinance, because the new appraised home value was less than the principal amount due on the original loan. The buyer would have to pay the difference in order to refinance. This wasn't possible for most people, so they were forced to continue paying the original loan. Many buyers were not able to meet the new monthly payment obligations and defaulted on their loans.

Another piece of the puzzle was the risky business lenders got into by allowing new and unqualified buyers to finance up to 100 percent of the purchase price of their homes. Buyers put nothing down! Lenders also failed to fully verify the income of some applicants. In order to increase profits, lenders were making as many loans as possible, even to buyers who would not qualify under normal circumstances.

This is the subprime market constantly discussed in the news. Lenders also got deeply involved with some creative financing options to meet a wide range of buyer needs. The popular loan, which I actually received, was the 80/20. To avoid forcing the buyer to pay private mortgage insurance (PMI), lenders would allow them to split the mortgage into two separate "piggyback" loans. The first was normally a fixed rate or ARM loan representing a conventional mortgage. The second was an equity line of credit with a variable interest rate from day one. The rate on the second loan was typically higher and covered the additional risk the lender assumed by not requiring PMI, or it covered PMI payments made by the lender. Depending on the rate and amount of the second loan, the payment could rise fairly significantly if the prime or other basis rate increased. This could happen immediately, as the second loan was a variable rate from the start. See, what people were doing was scraping together every penny they could find out of their monthly budget in order to buy the biggest home possible. Why not? This was a great time to buy, according to everyone in the industry. The tragic meltdown occurred once buyers' fixed rates expired on their primary loans and turned into variable rates or the prime rate increased on the second loan. Remember, they were scraping together everything they had, so buyers were not prepared for even the slightest increase in payments. Didn't someone tell these buyers that the payments would soon rise—and possibly by a significant amount? Didn't the lenders care to determine the buyers' ability to pay back the loans at the potential and sometimes inevitable higher rate? The ARM option works well for buyers whose income is expected to rise sharply over the next few years, as they are able to buy now versus waiting several years. It's also OK for buyers who can afford possible payment fluctuation in both good and bad times or buyers who will sell before the loan adjustment period. The ARM option is not good for buyers who are too leveraged or not expecting additional income in the near future.

Another scary piece of this mess was the infamous interest-only option. Some mortgages were combined with an interest-only payment option to ever further lower the initial payment. This is troubling and very scary! This is how most credit cards work. You normally only have to pay the minimum payment each month, with no pressure to pay down the principal balance. The minimum payment only covers accrued interest and doesn't put the slightest dent in the principal balance. This is a great option for some buyers but not most. The interest-only option further led to buyers' false sense of security and belief that they could manage the payment forever, or at least until they refinanced or sold their houses.

<u>Credit and Panic</u> – Any radio station, TV channel, Internet site, or water fountain conversation will likely include something about the current housing market and how it has affected the ability to get credit. I continue to hear the phrase "credit crunch." Why do I keep hearing the phrase credit crunch on the news? Who are the banks crunching? Other banks? Businesses? The public? Are they crunching the people or organizations that should be crunched? I don't see too much of an issue with banks tightening up on their lending standards. This is a good thing. Aren't lax lending standards what got us into this mess in the first place? Businesses and individuals who can't get credit probably shouldn't get credit. They may be too leveraged or unable to re-pay a loan. I actually just purchased a new car and had no problem getting an auto loan, so I'm not sure I agree with the credit crunch issue. The problem here is that everyone is in panic mode. And what happens when people are scared? Answer: They hold on to their money and stop buying the goods and services offered by businesses around the world. This is what is happening today. There is not much consumer confidence, as consumers are fearful of tomorrow. "Will I still have my job? Will I be able to put food on the table?" they wonder. These fears are a major cause of our economic crisis. Some fears are justified and very real, while others are inflated and unnecessary. No matter how good the economy

is, people will and should have concern for their future well-being. This is healthy and helps create a balance and promotes smart decision making. But until consumers begin feeling comfortable about tomorrow, they will not buy today.

I understand it can be difficult to control spending, and we all want things now, not later. But the thought that we depend so heavily on financing to fuel our economy is sometimes frightening. Where does all this money come from? Who0 is making these loans? What if they run out of money? What if borrowers on a mass scale can't pay back the loans? These are questions most people don't ask but are now asking since the credit crisis is becoming a hot topic.

My Personal Experience

So by now most of you are probably wondering how I got caught up in this mess. Like many others, I was an informed buyer who noticed the housing market boom and saw a golden opportunity to make a few bucks. I knew the risks but decided to play the game anyway. Some of the decisions I made were very risky and could have resulted in financial disaster.

It was the early part of 2002 when my wife and I decided to begin looking at houses. We weren't seriously looking but had a desire to get out of the town house we were renting. We had no experience in the housing market and didn't have a clue what we could afford. All we were familiar with was the amount we paid in rent each month and how we hated the fact that we were not building equity or accumulating any wealth. We had both recently graduated from college and decided it was time to begin looking for a house.

We began our search by driving in random neighborhoods searching for something—not sure what at the time. We were mainly looking at areas and neighborhoods, trying to decide where to narrow down the search. While driving around one weekend, we happened to stumble upon a newer development with a "model open" sign in front of the first house. We decided to walk in and look around. We met with the salesperson, who informed us that the current development was sold out, but they would soon begin selling lots in a new 125-home development across the street. He did not know the release date but told us to check back in a few months.

Well, a few months went by, and although we did continue looking in other areas and talking to other builders, nothing ever materialized. It wasn't until one Sunday afternoon while driving around a few neighborhoods that we decided to revisit the builder with the upcoming 125-house development. Ironically, the day we revisited they had just released thirteen lots. When we walked in, the salesperson greeted us and explained that thirteen lots had just been released on Wednesday, and only three lots remained. It so happened that the lot we liked the best was one of the first to go, but the deposit on it had been canceled earlier that morning, so it was one of the three lots still available. The salesperson told us that we only needed to put down a $500 deposit to hold the lot. The deposit was fully refundable, and the check wouldn't even be cashed until the new base prices were released in a few weeks and we decided to move forward. We knew the old pricing and had an idea where the new pricing would fall, but it was a bit nerve-racking not knowing what the exact base pricing would be or how much we could afford. Although we weren't convinced on the lot, we didn't see any risk in putting down a fully refundable deposit, so we gave him a check!

We spent the next few weeks reviewing our finances and trying to figure out what we could afford. We met with a mortgage banker, who helped with the process, and it was amazing how much we were told we could afford. We were approved to receive much more than we were comfortable spending. Based on our calculation, we would not have enough money for food if we maxed out our buying power. Coming from a long history of renting, we were not sure what was involved in buying a house. Fortunately, our first lender spent time helping us determine not only what we could afford but what we were comfortable spending. Once we figured out what we could afford, we decided to move forward with the process. We met with the salesperson and went through the tedious process of designing our new home. After many arguments, disagreements, tears, and roughly eight months, our new home was complete.

We moved into our newly built home in April of 2003. We ended up purchasing the home for $272,000. This included the base price of $235,000 and $37,000 in options. We were terrified that we were getting in over our heads and would end up broke. That was a lot of money for us at that time. We were both recent college grads, and this was by far the largest purchase we had ever made.

By the time we moved into our new home, the base price of our model had increased by approximately 10 percent. This was a 10 percent increase in an eight-month period. The wheels started spinning, so I began collecting base price sheets as the builder released each section of lots. I also started researching prices of other builders and prices of existing homes and continued to notice that prices were increasing at a fairly rapid rate. I also discovered that the demand for homes was very high, and existing homes were not sitting on the market very long. I knew several people in the market to buy who lost bids on a house even when they put in a bid over the asking price. It wasn't long before it struck me that we were sitting on a gold mine. We thought, could we have gotten lucky and just happened to buy at the right time? Was this price appreciation normal and here to stay? I didn't think this was normal and certainly questioned the rapid price increase but couldn't have been happier with the price appreciation on our home. On several occasions, we even noticed people camping out in front of the new model home, awaiting the next set of lots to be released. By the one-year mark, the base price of our model had climbed to over $300,000 with no end in sight.

We were thrilled with the amount of equity we were accumulating and decided to invest some of our recent profits. A friend of mine happened to be selling his town house in the city of Baltimore just at the time I was looking to invest some money. Naturally I wanted to dump it right back into the real estate market. The housing market in the city was booming. Prices were rising sharply, and demand was high. I was fairly familiar with the downtown housing market, and the town house for sale was in a perfect location. After a quick tour, we made the decision to purchase the town house and use it as rental property. In order to come up with the down payment, we applied for a second mortgage and received a large equity line of credit against our house. When we applied for the loan, we were surprised how easy it was. We were basically asked how much money we wanted to borrow, and ironically our house was appraised for that exact amount over our original purchase price. We used $65,000 from the equity line as a down payment on the rental property, which we purchased for $264,000. We quickly found a renter and became landlords. We only planned to hold the property for a few years and of course sell for a huge profit. We weren't too worried about the fact that we only collected enough rent to cover 80 percent of the mortgage payment, because we saw this as an investment. We figured the monthly loss would pale in comparison to the profits we would make. So we now had a house and a rental property that were both continuing to rise in value. We thought we were going to be rich!

With an investment property and our current home continuing to increase in value, you would think we would have been satisfied. We continued to study the market and watch home prices and demand rise. We were in a great area, and we had one of the best lots and one of the best homes in the neighborhood. Our first home was all we needed at the time, but we couldn't stop thinking about the money we could make by selling it. We also noticed the demand wave continuing to move north of us and wondered if we should try to buy ahead of the market in an effort to repeat the success we had on our first home. We debated for a while, but after living in the house for only eighteen months, we decided to sell. Instead of just cashing in our profits, we decided to use them to buy another house in hopes of making more money. Now the question was "Do we buy a bigger house or buy the same size?" Well, in an effort to maximize our return, we decided to buy a bigger one. Strange, huh? Not too much more than a year earlier, we were worried about affording our home, and now we were buying a bigger one even after we had just purchased a rental property. The plan was to buy a bigger house with a bigger yard to hopefully give us a bigger return on our investment. We planned to live there for only a few years and then sell it for a profit. Some people call this "flipping homes," but we thought we were sneaky and that no one else had caught on to this phenomenon. Little did we know this was happening all across the country in some fashion or another.

After we made the decision to sell our house and buy a bigger one, we began the all-too-familiar home search again. We picked out an area we thought was going to be the next hot spot. We quickly found a builder with available lots that were ready for building. We knew the process already, so we designed our new home in a short period of time and began preparing for the eventual move. We didn't want to have a transitional move while our new house was being built, so we decided to wait until after construction started to put our current home on the market. Once construction began on our new house, we put our current home on the market, and as expected, the house sold quickly. We had our first offer at 9:00 a.m. the very first morning it was on the market. It took less than one hour to sell our house! My Realtor was floored. She and I had debated about the asking price. I of course wanted more, and she wanted less. We ended up receiving an offer of $489,000. Keep in mind we had only paid $272,000 less than two years earlier.

The offer we received ended up falling through, and we received an additional two offers. We accepted the third offer for the asking price of $489,000. We turned a profit of $217, 000 in just two years!

Now the scary part. I often think of the word risky, and when I need a true definition, I just reflect on our decision to sell our first home and buy a bigger one. You see, we not only decided to sell our house and buy a bigger one, but we signed the contract and closed on the land before putting our first house on the market. At that point we were locked into the deal. The builder made the interest payments throughout the construction process and turned over the keys once the house was complete. For a five-month period of time we owned three houses! We were sitting on well over $1.5 million worth of real estate at that time. The slightest bit of miscalculation or bad luck, and we would have been doomed. Strangely, the builder and mortgage company were perfectly OK with all of this. You'll know what I mean when I tell you the purchase price. Our mortgage consisted of the ever-popular 80/20 five-year ARM with an interest-only option. This meant that we put nothing down and avoided PMI. Guess what? We also built the closing costs into the second loan. This meant that we had a 100-plus percent financed home. This may seem staggering, but I haven't even gotten to the scary part yet. The scary part was the fact that we purchased a 6,000-

square-foot home (including a three-car garage and unfinished basement) sitting on 4.69 acres for the bargain price of $736,000. Our plan was to ride the wave for a few years and sell the house for a big profit. Of course this would have worked if the market had continued to rise.

Before buying the new house, we calculated the maximum amount we could pay each month and built the biggest house we could afford. The more expensive the house, the bigger the profit, we thought. The funny thing was the lender and builder agreed. We financed the house through the builder's recommended lender. They both basically encouraged us to get in over our head. They couldn't have been happier.

We were definitely on a tight budget at first, but our finances were OK. We had just enough to get by. It wasn't until we had lived in the house for a few months that things started to change, and our worst fears came true. The first thing that happened was our renters in the city decided to break the lease and move out early. We received plenty of warning but weren't sure what to do. We could try to stop them or pursue legal action but felt we were better off trying to quickly find another renter. We certainly were not prepared to take on the additional mortgage payments. The second thing that happened was the interest rate on our equity line began to rise. As little as the increase was in comparison to the entire mortgage payment, we hadn't left much wiggle room in our initial calculation. We were now faced with a higher mortgage payment on our primary home and paying the entire mortgage on our rental property. We were terrified. We eventually found another renter, but we had to cover the mortgage payments for several months on our own. Fortunately, we were able to make ends meet through our rough patch.

Our ability to make ends meet was primarily due to our decision to create a rainy-day fund with some of the profits from the sale of our first home. We purposely set aside enough money to pay the mortgage on our rental property for up to eight months in case we had trouble finding a renter. We ended up using money from the fund to subsidize the mortgage payments on both homes. We also refinanced the equity line on our primary home after living there for six months in an effort to lower the payment. Not surprisingly, we had no problem getting our house reappraised for more than the purchase price. We were able to get a better rate and saved a little bit of money each month. Ultimately, it was our rainy-day fund that saved us from financial disaster.

Ironically, we only lived in our new home for ten months. After ten months, I was promoted within my company, and we relocated to Chicago. It was now time to sell again! We were sort of exited but also very nervous. At this point we hoped to just break even on the sale, but unfortunately things didn't work out in our favor. The house went on the market in late 2006, as the housing market was beginning to come down from its recent peak. We had lots of showings and interested buyers but no offers. Finally after eight months on the market, we received and eventually accepted our first offer and sold the house for $662,000. This equated to an estimated loss of $110,000. We had used some of the profits from our first home to build a deck, add landscaping, repaint the entire house, and make a few other upgrades, all of which added to the loss. Aside from the fact that we had purchased the house at a peak time in the market, we also hadn't done our homework when evaluating the area and actual property. One of the biggest complaints we received from potential buyers was the size of the property. We were very surprised to discover that a majority of people who looked at our house didn't want 4.6 acres of land. We were still in a neighborhood, but 4.6 acres wasn't as appealing to others as we had originally thought. When searching for property, we had also failed to recognize the significance of another housing development just a few miles away. We were located just a few miles from the largest housing development in the state of Maryland. The development was called Bulle Rock and was located in sight of the Chesapeake Bay and next to a top-rated golf course. The development consisted of several types of homes with multiple builders. It was a gated community with very small lots and maintenance-free landscaping. In my opinion, our house was not comparable to the homes in this development, but several people who looked at our house ended up buying a house in the Bulle Rock development. We were definitely right about the area, but I guess we were wrong about the house. The good news is the loss didn't bury us. Soon after my job transfer, we sold our rental property to the current tenant. We only made a small amount of money on the sale but gladly sold it when we did. The market was heading down and was very saturated with inventory by that time. With help from our rainy-day fund and the equity and profits from the sale of our rental property, we were able to pay off our loss and stay afloat.

So now you have a very quick snapshot of my personal experience with the housing market, credit crunch, cash flow, and other issues that plague us today. I can't tell you how important cash flow is in this or any economy. Taking risks is a necessary part of prosperity, but all risks need to be smart and calculated. I still to this day ask myself what I was thinking. I can somewhat come up with an answer, and it basically boils down to inexperience and my strong desire to get rich quick. I was new to the housing market and luckily got in and out at the right time. I just didn't have the sense to realize I was in way over my head. The only question I can't answer is what the mortgage company was thinking. They made a loan to us that clearly did *not* make sense. Based on our income, we should *not* have qualified for that loan. Were they in denial? Or were they just ignorant to the market conditions and trying to squeak out every bit of profit they could that year? I don't know the answer but have to imagine they have now had their fair share of home foreclosures and are possibly out of business.

Who's to Blame?

<u>Buyers</u> – Whenever something goes wrong, we ask ourselves, "Who's at fault? Whom should we blame?" I certainly asked these questions and many others after losing $110,000 on the sale of my third house. How could the market change so drastically in such a short period of time? We could debate the answer to this question all day long and never agree. We could ask one hundred market experts, economists, professors, or politicians and get a different answer every time. In my opinion, the fault ultimately lies in the hands of the buyer. People made decisions to buy homes they could not afford. These poor decisions are the root cause of the housing and economic crises we face today. Yes, buyers may have been influenced by another party with insincere motives, but buyers must hold themselves accountable. They made the decisions. They should have known the risks. They should have known the details of their loans. They should have studied the market and realized that the houses they were buying were significantly overpriced. Buyers, more than anyone, should have known what they could afford. Even while Wall Street got greedy,

lenders relaxed their standards, regulators stood by and watched the increased risk in the mortgage arena, the government reacted too slowly, builders continued to build and raise prices - the buyers kept on buying.

I was personally involved in this mess; therefore I cannot exclude myself from this group. Buyers were reckless. They were buying homes they could not afford. Since money was cheap, buyers concentrated on the monthly payment with little regard for the purchase price of their homes. With low rates, buyers were able to purchase more expensive homes and were duped by the industry into buying homes at escalated and outrageous prices. A sort of panic was created in which people thought they must buy immediately as prices were rising and get deals while they lasted. Buyers should have known that the housing market is cyclical and would eventually go down. Buyers should have known that home prices can't grow at those incredible rates and be expected to stay.

As I watched my first house skyrocket in value, I kept asking myself, "When will it stop?" I knew it wasn't normal and the price would have to come back down eventually. On the other hand, I thought it might continue rising and just hit a plateau and not come down. Did we possibly get lucky and just happen to buy at the right time? I began to fear I would never be able to afford another house again if the prices continued to rise. We actually considered selling our house and renting again so we could keep the profits and not risk losing them. Looking back now, that would have been a great idea, but unfortunately that didn't happen. We wanted more! And wanting more is what drove us to buy again and buy bigger. It's also what drove many others to do the same thing. Buyers failed to pay attention and made poor decisions. We helped create this mess and have no one to blame for it but ourselves. I understand that some buyers were misled, but when buying a house you need to do your homework. You need to ask questions, do your research, and understand what you are getting yourself involved in. If you get an ARM loan, you need to ask what might happen in a few years when the fixed rate becomes adjustable or the prime rate increases. It's very unfortunate that so many buyers claim no fault and blame the lender or government for their problems. People need to take responsibility for their own actions just as they are asking of lenders and the government.

Lenders – Lenders of course lend money for houses, cars, boats, business purchases, issue credit cards, and so forth. Credit is a very important part of our economy, as it allows people to buy things today that they would normally not have the ability or discipline to save up for. What it also does is allow people and businesses to spend beyond their means. Too many lenders got greedy and decided to lower their lending standards in order to make more loans and improve profits. Lowering their standards caused them to get sloppy and loan too much money to people who were unable to pay back the loans. They failed to truly evaluate the risk involved with some loans. Too many buyers were receiving loans for homes they just could not afford.

Lenders also offered too many risky loan programs to unqualified buyers. Lenders sold ARM and/or interest-only option loans to unqualified buyers. These loans were OK for the first few years but became major problems when the rates changed and the payments suddenly increased. Buyers found themselves unable to afford the new payment amounts and couldn't pay back the loans. Since buyers received more money than they could afford, they quickly became overextended and defaulted on their loans. These loan defaults started to occur at rapid rates and on a mass scale, which created a tidal wave of home foreclosures. This wave of foreclosures started our economic crisis.

Aggressive lending practices also created a larger than normal demand for homes. This increased demand led to explosive home building and price appreciation of new and existing homes. Everyone wanted to buy a house or move to a bigger one.

Lenders were lending money to almost anyone. A buzz was created, and a lot of people believed that *now* was the time to buy. Potential buyers were told that home prices were rising, so they should buy a house immediately while the prices were affordable and the rates were low. Loan officers were very good at convincing buyers to keep their money and finance 100 percent of their home, since rates were so low. This made the deal look better on paper for the short term but left the buyer and lender extremely vulnerable. It's OK for businesses and consumers to take risks, but taking these kinds of risks on a mass scale is a recipe for disaster. Too many lenders took advantage of buyers and led them to believe that the housing market was strong and they were better off not putting money down. This allowed buyers to take on too much debt. Lenders failed to explain the risks involved with interest-only, ARM, and 100-percent-financed mortgages. Shame on those lenders!

<u>Wall Street</u> – So you might ask why lenders were so eager to make these risky, unconventional, and subprime loans. One reason is Wall Street. Wall Street investors created an increased demand for mortgage-backed investment products. Lenders sold most of these subprime and risky mortgages to Fannie Mae and Freddie Mac, which repackaged the loans into mortgage-backed securities and made them available for sale to investors. This increased

demand caused lenders to lower their typical lending standards and make loans to unqualified buyers. Lenders were encouraged to hurry up and generate lots of mortgage loans to make available for investors to purchase. Although it was still the lenders' decision to lower their lending standards, Wall Street investors have a lot of influence, as most large companies are publicly owned and traded. The subprime mortgages were also thought to be low risk, as most were insured. The fact that they were insured would have minimized the risk in a good or normal market, but we were not in a normal market as lenders were originating and selling mass amounts of risky loans in the subprime market. Once these risky and subprime mortgages started failing, the fact that they were insured did not matter. The insurance companies were not prepared for mortgage defaults on the scale we have seen today. The mass quantity and rapid rate of home foreclosures ignited a wave of company failures. We began to see lenders, investment banks, insurance companies, and so forth fail.

As a society, we are focused on growth and prosperity. Growth is a key ingredient for success. If we are not growing, we are shrinking or failing by some standards. I tend to agree that growth is good and very necessary. Unfortunately, we have grown too fast. As a society, we were so focused on profits and "What can you do for me now?" that we forgot about the simple fundamental fact that "cash is king," and every business and individual person must have a positive cash flow position in order to survive. Our growth and profit efforts caused us to become too leveraged. We promoted and insisted on what we have *now* with little regard for the future. Wall Street created pressure for companies to perform and increase profits. Wall Street also saw the opportunity to profit from the mortgage business and increased its demand for mortgage-backed investment products, which in turn influenced lenders to make more risky loans.

Financial institutions (lenders and investors) were less concerned with how their company would look in five or ten years than how it looked today. Why wouldn't they be? If I were the CEO of a company and my compensation was based on the short-term profits I could show on paper today, you better believe that I would take risks in order to improve today's bottom line. Unfortunately, as we are now all aware, these bottom-line figures were delusional figures at best. They didn't consider the long-term risk involved or potential bad debt. How can someone be compensated if the result of their actions isn't known? When making loans, you obviously can't determine if the loan is good or bad until the loan fully pays off without any problems. When lenders were handing out 100-percent-financed loans in the subprime market, they should have known that future problems would exist. They influenced buyers to borrow as much as they could afford today. With some creative financing packages, they could help the buyer borrow more by lowering today's payment ... while of course ignoring tomorrow. Lenders offered three-year ARMs with interest-only payment options. What the lenders didn't do was discuss what the payment could be in three years and calculate the buyer's ability to pay if or when the payment increased. I assume some lenders didn't care because they knew it would be someone else's problem, or they planned to sell the mortgage to Wall Street investors anyway.

<u>Government</u> – So what role did the government play in the housing mess? In my opinion, the government failed in many areas that helped cause the housing market collapse. The first thing it did was fail to regulate the industry. Too many lenders were lending money outside of standard guidelines. Government regulators failed to step in and stop the lending frenzy. Too many lenders and other financial institutions were not regulated like typical banks, although they offered similar lending services. Another thing the government did was lower federal lending rates all the way down to 1 percent, which created a large source of "cheap money." When money is cheap, people will borrow—and borrow is what they did. The government also put lots of pressure on the industry

in the late 1990s and especially the government sponsored enterprises (GSEs) to expand mortgage loans to low- and moderate-income borrowers. This helped create the easing of credit standards, which led to an increased number of mortgages in the subprime market. The overall intervention and influence of the government is believed by some to have started the entire housing and economic crisis we are in today.

I strongly believe in the free enterprise system. Without it, we lose the basic motivation needed to drive the economy. Even though the free enterprise system is great, it still needs to have rules, just like laws are needed to protect our freedom. Most people seem to confuse the role of the government and its need to support the free market. We need the government to govern and regulate, not control and operate the economy. The role of the government should be to balance the needs and interests of America in support of a common goal. The government should have seen this coming and stepped in to create guidelines to help slow down the explosive and unhealthy growth. It should have also created more guidelines for some mortgage lenders and investment banks not currently regulated. Everyone was already questioning when the housing market bubble would burst. I think everyone knew it would happen sooner or later, but what puzzles me is why nothing was done by the government until after it burst and our economy started to suffer. How did the government regulators not see this coming and step in to regulate? Government regulators allowed banks and mortgage lenders to originate too many risky loans, which helped lead to the housing meltdown. Were the government regulators on vacation for the past few years?

Of course everyone has heard the recent news about the two government-sponsored mortgage companies Fannie Mae and Freddie Mac. They both failed because they were too leveraged and did not have enough cash to weather the storm caused by the housing market collapse. Fannie Mae and Freddie Mac are the largest purchasers of mortgages in the secondary market and helped lead to some of the loose lending standards. They were buying most of the subprime mortgages from lenders who originated the loans and then reselling them as investment securities. They obviously did not research the mortgages they were buying and properly determine the level of risk. Could this be due to the pressure from the government to increase the amount of subprime loans? Fannie Mae and Freddie Mac are actually publicly owned companies. I would say sorry to the stockholders, but since the companies are GSEs, the American taxpayers could be liable for bad debts to the extent of several hundred billion dollars when problems exist. Fannie Mae and Freddie Mac are certainly very important to the mortgage industry, as they free up needed capital for lenders to use to make additional loans. This helps fuel the economy by allowing buyers to continue buying homes at affordable rates. The issue isn't the existence of these GSEs but the way in which they recently conducted business in an effort to appease the government and make a profit for shareholders. These GSEs must make a better effort to truly evaluate loan risk and have strict guidelines to limit the amount of risk they can assume.

I don't follow politics very closely or know too much about the details of government intervention and how it can affect the marketplace but did find it odd that the Federal Reserve continued to lower rates even when the economy seemed to be doing quite well. The Federal Reserve seemed to be encouraging additional spending at a time when we were spending too much. The housing market was exploding while rates continued to fall. The federal funds rate dipped all the way down to 1 percent in 2003; the federal funds rates is a rate that influences many other lending rates. I was certainly happy to receive a great interest rate on my home but couldn't believe the rates were hitting record lows in a time of massive expansion. I always believed one goal of the Federal Reserve Bank was to raise and lower federal lending rates in an effort to help balance the economy. Shouldn't rates have been increased during the incredible housing boom? Wouldn't this have slowed the growth and created tighter lending standards?

The Solution

In order to fix our economy, we must first determine who controls it. Is it the government? Is it businesses? No. It's people! Everyday people control the economy, people who buy goods and services offered by businesses around the world. These simple actions ignite the cylinders of our economy. When it comes to the housing market, buyers make the decisions to buy or not to buy. It's that simple. When buyers buy under normal circumstances, it will most likely lead to a healthy and balanced economy. When buyers buy under abnormal circumstances, such as the past few years, it creates an unhealthy environment. To fix this, we must go back and make fundamental changes to the root of the problem.

<u>Buyers</u> – First and foremost, buyers must prove to themselves and to lenders that they have adequate disposable income to purchase a home. Home foreclosures are too much of a burden on our economy to be taken lightly. Buyers must ask questions and know exactly what they are getting themselves into when purchasing homes. Know the rates, know the market, and know what you can

afford. No one knows your spending habits better than you. Sit down and determine where your money actually goes. You might be surprised what you spend your money on and how it's proportionate to your total disposable income. You must create a realistic budget and figure out not only what you have to spend on a home but what you are *willing* to spend. Don't guess or estimate. You may not be willing to lower your standard of living by giving up certain activities in order to pay for your new home. You will want to discover this before buying a house, not after.

Another thing buyers need to do is admit when they're in trouble. Talk to your lender. The lending company might be willing to help. Don't dodge the phone calls or collection letters. This will only make matters worse. Lenders do not want to kick you out of your home—not because they like you, but because they will lose money. You may be able to bargain with them and renegotiate a new loan that's more affordable to you. It's not only in your best interest to talk to the lender, but it's also in their best interest to talk to you.

As a society we need to adjust the way we think about borrowing and spending. Our spending habits need to change. Manageable debit is OK and in most cases good. We need to be careful and not let credit allow us to spend beyond our means. We need to create a better balance between what we buy today versus what we wait for and buy tomorrow. Remember, what you buy today on credit will limit what you can afford to buy tomorrow. Consider limiting loans to the short term and avoid long-term loans for materialistic or nonessential purchases. Keeping loans short will decrease the risk of getting in trouble. With a long-term loan you are stuck with the burden to pay it off for many years to come. Your needs or financial situation can change at any time and limit your ability to pay off the loan. Of course when buying something like a house, you will need a long-term loan. Make sure to calculate your ability to make the loan payments now and in the future. Without a good balance you will tie up all of your cash and hit the purchasing ceiling. When this happens, you are no longer able to buy again until you pay off yesterday's purchases. How much will it actually hurt you to save up for that new TV versus putting it on your credit card and paying for it over the next few years? Think about it: if you wait just a few months and save up for the TV, you can buy it free and clear and not penalize your future. All it takes is small, short-term sacrifices. Long-term prosperity is worth the wait.

Adjustable Rate Mortgages – Adjustable rate mortgages have gained tremendous popularity recently due to the lower up-front rate and initial payment. These loans are great for some buyers and extremely risky for others. They are great for buyers whose income is expected to rise or buyers who expect to be in their homes for only a short period of time. Buyers expecting to move before the expiration of the fixed rate may not face the loan adjustment period. ARMs are not so great for buyers on a relatively fixed income level, whose income is not expected to grow much. Buyers in this case may be unable to afford payment increases that may result from higher interest rates. In order to minimize the risk of problems, there must be guidelines to determine who is eligible to receive an ARM. Buyers not meeting specific guidelines should only be eligible to receive fixed-rate mortgages. Most buyers need to be able to predict expenditures through consistent monthly mortgage payments in order to prevent defaulting on their mortgages.

<u>Interest-Only Payment Options</u> – Any loan with an interest-only payment option should follow similar if not stricter guidelines as the guidelines for ARM loans. The lower initial payment can give buyers a false sense of what they can afford. This can get uninformed or unqualified buyers in trouble. Interest-only options should only be used for buyers with high expectations of income growth or buyers with irregular income schedules, such as a commissioned salesperson. They may also be good for buyers expecting to move before the adjustment period. Buyers not meeting these criteria should

not receive this option, as they may be faced with negative or reverse equity as a result of not paying off any of the principal loan amount when they are making only the minimum interest payments.

Down Payment – All buyers should put down at least 5 percent of the purchase price of any home. Of course the more you put down, the lower the risk. This is especially important if you only plan to stay in the home a short period of time. If you're in your home only a short period of time, you may not have much price appreciation, and even worse, the value of your home could go down. If the value goes down, you may have to come up with a large chunk of cash in order to sell your house! Keep in mind when selling a house you need to consider taxes, Realtor fees, and other closing costs that can add up to a significant amount of money. You may need to sell it for up to an estimated 10 percent more than what you paid for it just to break even. A 10 percent price appreciation in a short time frame is not likely under normal market conditions. Without at least 5 percent down, you significantly increase your risk of taking a loss on a short sale. I certainly understand the difficulty some will face in coming up with this amount of money, but this is only a recommendation to lower the risk involved for the buyer. If you plan to stay in your home for a long period of time, you may not benefit as much from putting down 5 percent. You may be OK with a 100-percent-financed loan, but in my opinion you will lower your risk by putting down something.

<u>Fixed-Rate Mortgages</u> – Fixed-rate mortgages are the safer bet for most buyers. With a fixed-rate mortgage, you are able to estimate your monthly payment with a fair degree of certainty. Some things like taxes and insurance may fluctuate but most likely by small amounts. Any first-time, high-risk, or marginally qualified buyer should receive a fixed-rate mortgage. The inability of some buyers to budget and predict their monthly payments is what started our housing crisis and must not be repeated. I think a great step in minimizing mortgage foreclosures is requiring more fixed-rate mortgages.

<u>Piggyback Loan/PMI</u> – The popularity of the piggyback loan is mainly due to PMI. To avoid forcing buyers with less than 20 percent equity to pay PMI, lenders will give them two separate loans and build the PMI payments or risk into the interest rate. The first loan normally covers 80 percent of the total loan and is a fixed rate or ARM. The second, or piggyback loan, covers 10, 15, or 20 percent, depending on how much the buyer puts down. The second loan is typically an adjustable rate from day one that's much higher than the rate on the first loan. The interest paid on this loan accounts for the level of risk involved with the fact that the buyer has less than 20 percent equity. I have not priced

nor paid PMI, but from what I can tell, it doesn't favor the buyer. PMI is a needed resource to help lenders spread out losses due to failed mortgages, but I feel that PMI premiums should be paid by the lender and charged back to the buyer through the interest rate. If the lender decides to insure the loan, I imagine it would be at a much better rate. The net result to the buyer should be a lower payment. There's also no reason why both loans can't be at a fixed rate to help create more stability in loan payments.

Rainy-Day Fund – This is sometimes tough to do, but more people need to do everything possible to create a rainy-day fund to help out in times of financial need. No one knows what the future will look like, but for most of us it involves paying bills, and you can't pay the bills when you're out of money. You never know when you will lose your job, need to make repairs to your house, make repairs to your car, suffer financial loss, and so forth and need to spend more than what's coming in the door. Having quick access to a small pool of funds will help you in times of need. There are many debates about how much you should set aside, but the more you save, the better. You may also need to reevaluate your standard of living if you are unable to create a savings account and put away money each month. This could be an indicator that you are living beyond your financial means. Our family's decision to set aside funds really saved us in our time of need.

<u>First-Time Buyers</u> – There should be regulations requiring all first-time home buyers to be employed for more than one year before being eligible for a home loan. This would not be required with a qualified cosigner. We all know how uncertain our financial situation is in the first few years of a career, and especially in the very first year. Requiring all first-time buyers to wait at least a year will help buyers figure out what their disposable income will be and how much of a mortgage payment they can afford. A potential buyer just graduating from high school or college will likely encounter many unexpected challenges with their finances. The goal is to protect them and their future financial well-being.

<u>Lenders</u> – In order to minimize the chances of another housing crisis similar to what we face today, lenders must improve their lending standards and offer appropriate mortgage loan options to buyers. Only qualified buyers should receive home loans and for only the amount they can afford. Lenders must be responsible and not hand out cash to any willing party. It's hard to believe how easy it was not too long ago to get a loan for an overpriced home that you couldn't afford. Lenders are supposed to be specialists in their field and should have known better

than to loan money to people who couldn't afford to pay them back. Hopefully, they learned their lesson and will improve the customer evaluation process. Improving lending standards is very necessary to prevent this situation from occurring again. We will always have economic ups and downs, but home foreclosures on a mass scale are detrimental to the economy. Lenders must ask questions to determine the actual amount the buyer can afford. Standard debt-to-income ratios are a good starting point, but every buyer's spending habits are different. A home purchase is typically the largest purchase anyone ever makes. It's the lenders' job to provide customer service to buyers and help them through the process.

Lenders must also be willing to renegotiate loans if the buyer is unable to pay the mortgage. If the ARM rate expires and the payment suddenly increases, this may create an impossible situation for the buyer. Forget about the fact that the buyer may have been negligent or irresponsible; the lender must be willing to make business decisions and renegotiate loans. Some buyers may have been very responsible but just ran into unexpected financial trouble. How much does it cost a bank to foreclose on a home? According to Freddie Mac, the average cost of a home foreclosure is $60,000. I imagine the cost greatly increases when the housing market is in a down cycle. I think it's in everyone's best interest to renegotiate and keep people in their homes. It's to the lender's benefit to sit down and work out a new deal if possible.

<u>Public Companies</u> – We have seen many major public companies go under recently, and surprisingly, the CEOs of some companies had made fortunes in the previous years. It's interesting how the appearance of outstanding performance and high earnings can line executives' pockets one year while the company folds the year after? The boards of directors, CEOs, and other key executives of publicly held companies must be held accountable for their actions. They should be rewarded for good long-term performance, not short-term quarterly profits. They need to be held accountable to the same degree as the owner of a private company. If the company doesn't make money, the executives don't make money. I should also define money as *cash*. Executives cannot be paid solely on profits each fiscal year, as profits can be easily distorted. A company must have cash and make cash.

How is it that the executives of bankrupt public companies walk away with millions of dollars while the *owners* lose everything? Seems strange, huh? As investors we must demand accountability, fairness, and adequate compensation for our financial investment in the company. I completely understand and agree with the fact that great executives need to be rewarded for great performance. This is the only way to attract, retain, and promote the best. I know I certainly want the best CEO running each company I invest in! But what if there were no large payouts, and no golden parachutes? Would these companies collapse? I doubt it, but why can't public companies incentivize their executives with the same reward sought out by the owners of the company? Why shouldn't a CEO pay the price when times are bad? We suffer; why shouldn't they?

Executives should be paid in a similar fashion as the owners of the company. In the case of a public company, that would be the stockholders, you and I. We are paid in dividends. We can also make money based on the value of our stock but won't realize a gain until the shares are sold. Company executives decide how much of a dividend to pay out each quarter or fiscal year and the ability to pay dividends is typically a true representation of a company's actual performance. If executive bonuses, payouts, and pay increases were all in the form of or related to the percentage of dividend payouts, I think this would change executives' perspective. It would force them to operate the business in the best interest of the owners, which is you. There is no doubt that company executives will and should make a lot of money. They are in their position for a reason. Most have proven themselves to be worthy leaders capable of maximizing shareholder wealth, and they must be compensated accordingly. Without high compensation there is less motivation for greatness. Again, by no means am I saying that executives shouldn't make a lot of money. They should. We just need to make sure that the amount of money they make is a true representation of the individuals' and companies' actual long-term performance and is proportionate to the owners' share. Why should an executive receive more compensation proportionate to the owner? That doesn't make sense.

Wall Street also seems to be too concerned with the stock price and not very concerned with a company's true value. I think a stock's value should be determined by the company's current financial position, future outlook, and the dividend payout. You don't hear much about dividends in comparison to the actual stock price. To me it appears that stockholders reap the rewards mainly when they sell the stock for more than they paid for it. This phenomenon seems to have created most of the craziness in the stock market today. The stock market seems to consist of a giant group of day traders who falsely influence the value of stocks. Some say the increasing number of some risky and shortsighted hedge funds is helping to create this negative influence on stock prices. We are too concerned with stock price appreciation and not concerned enough with the dividend payout and long-term company value. Yes, stock price appreciation is great, but it's not the only way we can make a return on our investments. We need to demand more rewards along the way, and this may be possible if executive pay is tied more directly to dividends and long-term performance. The bottom line is executives' compensation can't be solely based on short-term profits. Their compensation must be tied to long-term outlook and performance and tied more directly to the percent received by the owners.

Most of the companies that recently failed due to the housing crisis are publicly held and partly responsible for causing the situation to begin with. Maybe if these company executives had been held to a higher standard or compensated differently, this crisis would not have occurred.

<u>Government</u> – I think everyone can agree that the government has a responsibility to regulate and help balance the U.S. economy in an effort to best serve the U.S. taxpaying citizens. The infamous question is how? Is it more regulation, more taxes, less taxes, government bailouts, government takeovers, or more government programs? I certainly don't have the answer, as our government and our economic markets are very complex and tied to various people and businesses all around the world. There are millions of businesses, cultures, governments, and individuals, all competing for self-preservation

and prosperity. No one knows exactly how each part or piece relates to another or how one person's actions affect another. Many people are currently voicing their opinions and taking action to help get us out of our current economic crisis. Although most people's intentions are correct, the result of their actions may not be.

In order to fix this mess, we need to start with the initial problem, which seems to be the collapse of the housing market. As I discussed previously, too many buyers were purchasing homes they could not afford, too many lenders were lending money to people who could not pay them back, too many investors were purchasing toxic mortgage-backed securities, and of course our government provided a cheap source of money to fund it all. Our government officials must do what we pay them to do and regulate the housing industry and overall economy. They must create guidelines for lenders, buyers, investors, builders, and other parties involved with the housing market. This market affects everyone in some form and is a big part of the U.S. economy. Regulation efforts should be designed to promote up-front prevention of problems and to create solutions to problems when they occur. The government must also be smarter with federal lending rates and adjust them in an effort to help create stability within our economy.

The government must be careful to regulate without overstepping its bounds though. I am very leery of too much government intervention. It seems to me the government steps in too often when it shouldn't and fails to step in when it should. Sometimes the government needs to sit back and let the free market work. Too much government intervention can actually backfire and negatively influence the economy. We are definitely in uncharted territory with our current economic and financial situation as we have seen with recent steps taken by the federal government to help troubled companies and industries. In addition to other rescue or bailout packages, the recent $700 billion bailout package for the financial industry is quite scary to me, even though I really don't know much about the details. Everyone seems to be demanding a quick fix to our economic problems, but I don't think that's possible. We are rushing to make decisions, and when we rush, we normally don't think things through, which can lead us to make poor decisions. The $700 billion may help stabilize the market today but at what cost to our future well-being? Are we penalizing ourselves tomorrow in order to make things better today? Are we creating a situation where we become too dependent on the government? At what point have we borrowed more than we can pay back? Are we "printing money," issuing debt to pay off debt? Are we creating mass inflation by pumping too much "extra" money into the economy? If we are issuing debt to fund the intervention, is this hurting other companies' ability to collect money from investors and lowering overall stock prices? Is the government creating a smaller investing pool by channeling money to failing companies? Would we be better off letting those failing companies suffer their losses like everyone else? Does giving them a financial boost magically solve their problems and improve the economy? Would the markets be better served with weaker companies failing and stronger companies taking over? How does the government decide what companies or industries to bail out and what companies not to bail out? I would imagine every company is important to the economy. Why not bail out everyone? It appears that the U.S. government has become an insurance company to troubled businesses.

As I continue to watch the current economic events unfold, I can't stop asking questions about what the government is doing with my money. Why is the government getting involved and bailing out so many companies? Is throwing money at problems always the best solution? Is a bailout really going to address the root cause of the problem? Is a bailout going to do anything to help increase consumer spending? Unless the government can find a way to increase consumer spending, a shrinking market will continue to shrink. The bailouts and rescue packages are getting out of control. Where does the government draw the line? When have we loaned out too much? I understand we are in tough times, but the government won't make things better by taking money from hurting taxpayers and giving it to failing companies. We will all have to suffer through these tough economic times in a natural and healthy way. I believe our economy should be based on the survival of the fittest principal. This is how we get the best of the best each company has to offer. Don't spend taxpayer dollars subsidizing weaker or failing companies. Some of these companies should be allowed to fail. If they don't fail, we will slow down natural economic progression as weaker companies are erroneously allowed to continue operating. I suffered my loss for my poor decisions, so why shouldn't they? Where was my bailout package? I say let companies compete, and the strongest will prevail. The strongest will prevail because they have the best people working for them who make the best decisions and offer the best goods and services. The public will agree and buy more of their goods and services. Let's take the three largest, the "Big Three" U.S. automakers, for example. Why is the government providing a bailout package for them? From what I can tell, the American public already decided not to bail them out by not buying enough of their cars. They also failed to bail themselves out when they knew they were in trouble.

The problem with the Big Three automakers is I just don't think giving them a blank check is a good idea. My fear with just giving them money is that it won't help in the long term, which needs to be the primary focus. A bailout will certainly help them in the short term but only to pay off debt. It appears the Big Three are asking for assistance in order to pay off debt and fund the current broken operation. I don't know all the reasons why the Big Three are in more debt and worse financial shape than other U.S. companies, but it's clear that the Big Three are not competitive in the marketplace and behind the times in many areas. It seems that they have failed to meet current consumer demands, as foreign competitors are gaining market share very quickly. They have profitability problems that some blame on the automakers' inefficient business model, slow reaction to the ever-changing market, excessive number of dealerships, poor reputation for vehicle reliability, and on the United Automobile Workers (UAW) for their enormous and uncompetitive payroll and health-care costs. The UAW has been a hot topic of debate recently, but in my opinion, labor unions can penalize both the worker and the company. Labor unions seem to remove performance measurements or incentives from most labor contracts. Doing this ultimately lowers productivity or the ability to reward productivity. Unions also seem to hold employers hostage in order to receive what may be unfair or uncompetitive wages and benefits for their members. Workers end up getting penalized as they are paid a flat, uniform wage and don't receive extra compensation for above-average performance. This obviously helps low performers and hurts high performers.

Are we worried about American jobs? Bailout or not, the U.S. automakers will be forced to lay off workers, as I don't think they will notice an increase in sales anytime soon. If U.S. automakers lay off workers, those workers will need to innovate and find new jobs. When one door closes, another door opens. The elimination of one job leads to the creation of another. This is how the economy works. This is what I call natural and healthy progress as the autoworkers now have the opportunity to join industries that are growing and possibly in need of additional labor such as information technology, Internet, health care, or possibly another U.S. automaker selling more cars. I certainly don't believe the American taxpayer should be responsible for saving any lost jobs. The American taxpayers are too worried about saving their own jobs! The argument that an auto bailout is needed for the workers just doesn't make sense. I believe the workers will be better off if the company is allowed to fail and forced to reorganize. If they don't reorganize soon, many more, or even all workers of the Big Three U.S. Automakers may be at risk of losing their jobs; and it's clear the companies are not able or willing to reorganize on their own. When people voice concern about "the worker," I think what they are actually saying is the overall U.S. worker and workforce. The government can't prevent or stop every job loss with every company nor should it. The government's goal should be to help protect, save, and create jobs in the *overall* U.S. workplace, *not* just at one company. Even if the Big Three suffer setbacks, the U.S. consumer market won't be reduced. Consumers will continue buying cars that meet their needs, and this will still help create new American jobs. Would the workers be better served working for a failing or thriving company? Would other, stronger companies and workers get hurt by the government artificially keeping the failing company alive? Is this bad for the economy, as we may suffer technological and innovative setbacks because weaker companies are kept in business, preventing the stronger competitors from thriving? Our current market clearly cannot support everyone who was in business yesterday, as the market today has been significantly reduced. By pumping up failing companies, the government may inadvertently cause the failure of a stronger company that under normal circumstances would outlast the weaker company and remain in business. This will ultimately cause a setback for America and its workers.

I also hear the automakers complaining about the credit market and its effect on consumer spending. They are complaining that the credit markets are still frozen and the lenders are not making loans. I don't buy this excuse, because as I stated earlier, I just purchased a new car and had no problem getting a loan. I think everyone is confusing yesterday with today. Today lenders are smarter with their lending standards, which is good for the economy. Yesterday's standards are not acceptable, as we all know where they got us.

Regardless of the reasons, the Big Three seem to have been in trouble for quite a while but have not taken steps to right-size or adjust their business model to meet current market conditions. Over the past few months, they should have taken drastic measures to scale back their operation and reduce costs like many other companies have already done. What were they waiting for? Even if they receive a bailout package, I have not heard how they plan to use the funds to immediately cut costs or increase sales. Unless they can quickly do either of the two, a bailout won't help. Maybe the best solution is to let the automakers file Chapter 11 and reorganize their businesses. The companies won't vanish; they will get a chance to readjust their business structures in order to create viable long-term operations. Or they could be acquired by another company or management group; then possibly smarter people would take over and fix the current problems the companies are having and actually save U.S. jobs. The reorganization efforts should be designed to make the companies more efficient, competitive, and innovative in order to sell more cars and make more money in the long run. This can't be achieved with a bandage fix in the form of a bailout, as it won't solve any long-term problems. My guess is the automakers will end up asking for more money again next year or possibly fail anyway. I wonder if the government gave a bailout package to the ice delivery companies in the 1920s after refrigerators were invented?

I don't mean to sound unsympathetic, as I certainly understand the importance of the U.S. auto industry and worker to our economy. I just don't believe a government bailout is the best course of action for the automakers. No one wants to see a section of the United States suffer, but we are all suffering in today's economy and all operating under the same conditions. Some have just made better decisions in the past or are making better decisions today that will keep them alive and set them apart from others. Although I don't support an auto bailout, I actually don't have a problem with the government using taxpayer dollars to help companies or industries in need if something dramatic and unexpected happens to them and the benefits help the economy as a whole. The use of government funds to help the airlines after 9/11 is a good example. Providing tax incentives to produce more fuel-efficient cars may also be a good idea. This will help the environment and may help the overall U.S. economy by reducing our purchases of foreign oil and providing more money available to circulate in the U.S. marketplace.

The ultimate question we have to answer is to what extent should the federal government step in to help struggling companies? Is the role of the government to decide what companies stay in business and what companies don't? Keep in mind that the Big Three are losing money because they are not making enough on their own and are majorly in debt. Is it really wise to give them your hard-earned money to possibly lose? That's like giving an overextended homeowner a loan to buy a second house. It will just put them further into debt and without a plan to increase their cash flow position. Money will certainly help pay off debt for some companies, but will it really affect consumer decisions? This is the real question that needs to be answered. That's what drives the economy, the decisions made by you and me. Are bailouts even fair to other suffering companies that may not receive assistance? I'm sure there are plenty of companies in other industries that went out of business recently that would have benefited from some type of government intervention. I'm sure there are many small businesses that are struggling and would greatly benefit from a government bailout. Why not help them? Collectively, they may be more important and influential to the economy than the automakers. Don't small businesses account for two-thirds of all businesses in the United States? Instead of offering a bailout to the current U.S. automakers, why not support and embrace the apparent decision already made by the U.S. consumer and offer tax credits or other incentives to bring in new, flourishing automakers to help keep U.S. production strong and actually save and/or create American jobs by increasing sales for products made in the United States. Or would the U.S. economy, workforce, and taxpayers be better off with the government not spending this money at all and giving everyone a tax credit? By giving everyone a tax credit, the public could choose where to spend the funds. I am much more in favor of tax breaks or incentives than the government collecting more taxes and letting government officials decide where to spend my hard-earned money. Or, rather than give a tax credit, the government could spend more on health care, education, law enforcement, roadway repairs and upgrades, or enhancements to our public transportation system. Either way, wouldn't this also save and create jobs?

We need to figure out how to build more American wealth and put more money to work in the U.S. economy. We also need to figure out how to create more jobs. The government can certainly take steps to help by lowering taxes in certain areas, offering tax incentives to select businesses, or reducing government bureaucracy or wasteful spending and using more money for roads, public transportation, and so forth. The government won't help by just giving money to failing companies. Giving money to failing companies won't create jobs, and creating more jobs is what's needed to turn the economy around.

As I said in the beginning, it's all about *cash*. The problems we face today are a result of too many people and businesses focusing on the short term and assuming too much debt. Everyone keeps talking about the need to help homeowners or help the workers, but the government can't do that by loaning out mass amounts of money. One of the reasons companies are failing is because they are poorly run or they are too leveraged! Putting them more in debt is not a good idea and certainly won't help the worker or the economy. These failing companies need to take a step back, reorganize, and work to create a more positive cash flow position. Letting companies fail is sometimes good for the economy, as it relieves the burden on stronger competitors and strengthens the market. This is how the free market works. Government intervention can negatively alter this and make a bad situation worse. The bailouts can actually have adverse affects and hurt more than they help. They slow down the ever-changing economy. The government is using taxpayer money to slow down natural economic progress.

Summary

The challenges we face today are not new; they are just different. We must not let panic fuel quick decisions that may not help us in the long run. We are in a recession, and some say headed for a depression, but pumping taxpayer dollars into select companies isn't always the answer. Let's face it; the taxpayers have no more to give! The government won't increase the size of a shrinking market by injecting funds into failing companies. This might only make the fall worse. The government can't create wealth by transferring taxpayer dollars to failing companies. You may temporarily help the failing company and worker but at the cost of hurting taxpayers and the overall economy. Too much of this, and now the taxpayer is in trouble and needs a bailout!

We must get back and address the fundamental things that control our economy. There are many factors that influence our economy, but consumer spending ultimately has the largest influence, and right now consumers are not spending. We need to figure out how to make them spend again and spend wisely. My guess is that we will be in a rebuilding period (recession, depression, call it what you want) for a few years while all necessary losses are satisfied and businesses and consumers regain control of their finances and accumulate more cash wealth. Once people accumulate the desired amount of cash wealth, they will begin spending again, and the economy will begin to turn around for the better. The days of financing everything or overextending ourselves are gone. Is the answer government intervention, smarter business decisions, smarter buying decisions, or time? Well I think the answer is all of the above. We must reflect on our recent mistakes and make better choices moving forward. We must also understand that the economy is cyclical, and we must be patient and give the free market time to adjust. We cannot jump into panic mode and make decisions that help in the short term but hurt in the long term. The government can help but is not capable of saving the economy by trying to manipulate the free market. Money doesn't grow on trees. We must let the free market work, and the strongest companies and people will prevail. We are all free to make decisions that affect our future, and the ones who make the wisest decisions or bring the most value to society will most likely prosper the most. This is good for our economy. This motivates us to be better.

As I said in the beginning, I'm no expert. I was directly involved in the housing market rollercoaster ride and learned some valuable lessons. I'm providing a few ideas that I think would help prevent the housing market and economy from getting into another situation like it's in today. I also raised quite a few questions in an effort to make people think, as I certainly don't have all the answers. My ideas are from my perspective and based on my own experiences and opinions so naturally may be very different from yours. I'm sure I missed a few details, but my goal is to help spark some interest in creating a better way of doing things in the future.

NOTES